CW01637174

BREAKTHROUGH TO LEARNING
LINGUISTICS IN THE SERVICE OF MAINSTREAM EDUCATION

Mary Mason and Bob Mason

University of Central England
Faculty of Education Papers

Issues in Education series: No. 2

Trentham Books

First published in 1997 by Trentham Books Limited

Trentham Books Limited
Westview House
734 London Road
Oakhill
Stoke-on-Trent
Staffordshire
England ST4 5NP

British Cataloguing in Publication Data
A catalogue record for this book is available from the British Library
ISBN: 1 85856 071 3

Designed and typeset by Trentham Print Design Ltd., Chester
and printed in Great Britain by Bemrose Shafron Ltd., Chester

Foreword

This is the second in the series of papers on issues in education to be published by the Faculty of Education at UCE. In it Mary Mason and Bob Mason explain the thinking that underlies their innovative approach to developing language skills in schools.

Mary Mason has had a long association with the Faculty of Education at UCE, first as a senior lecturer here and, after her retirement, as a Visiting Research Fellow. Her research into the linguistic features of academic language – the sort of language that is needed if pupils are to realise their potential in the school curriculum – resulted in the production of extensive teaching materials which were published as the Wigan Language Project. The materials were systematically trialled from 1984 to 1990 at Shevington High School, Wigan, where Bob Mason was the headteacher from 1974-90. They proved remarkably successful in improving GCSE results, and were subsequently revised by Mary Mason and published as *Breakthrough to Learning.* (They are available from the Business Development Unit, Wigan and Leigh College, PO Box 53, Parson's Walk, Wigan WN1 1BR. Tel: 01942 501536).

This paper presents the most extended and up-to-date explanation of the linguistic theory on which the *Breakthrough to Learning* approach is based in a way that is designed to be of practical value to all teachers and educationists concerned with language development across the secondary school curriculum.

Dr Richard Hatcher
Director of Research, Faculty of Education, University of Central England

Abstract

This study is based on the hypothesis that the explicit teaching of the linguistic features of Academic English will improve performance at G.C.S.E. across the curriculum.

However, if one's aim is to raise academic standards, a dilettante teaching of interesting facts about language is not enough: the description of the *relevant* features of academic language has to be available and the appropriate teaching methods used.

The hypothesis was tested by the authors during the period 1984-90 with dramatic results in terms of G.C.S.E. results. These results are brought up to date, together with the preliminary results of using the materials with bilingual pupils.

The theory on which the work in school was based was correct but inadequate. The present paper explains a development of the theory in terms of the functions of academic language, which the authors have recently put together. It demonstrates that, while we organise our everyday lives in terms of stories, academic language is organised in terms of variables and systems.

The paper is written for teachers and educationists who wish to understand the linguistic basis of the Wigan Language Project and its subsequent developments. The main points are contained in the body of the article and the detailed linguistic analysis is available in the Appendices. A glossary of linguistic terms is appended.

Contents

Linguistics

A man that looks on glass,
On it may stay his eye;
Or, if he pleaseth, through it pass,
And then the heav'n espy.
George Herbert

Language is like glass: we look *through* it to perceive the world beyond. Language is as natural to the human being as breathing: we take it for granted.

A linguist *stays his eye* on the glass. It is his/her task to analyse the various levels of language, devising systems which best describe how each works.

Note that throughout this paper, we shall be using the word 'linguist', not in the lay sense of a person who knows several languages, but to describe a scholar who is engaged in the scientific study of language in general. Usually this second kind of linguist does know several languages – languages are, after all, the raw material of Linguistics – but learning languages is by itself not his trade.

Nor is it the modern scientific linguist's business to prescribe the variety of language which people should speak or write, so as to be socially acceptable. An older generation of English teachers used their limited knowledge of 'grammar' to train pupils to write in the Standard English dialect rather than in their local dialects (for example, Fowler, 1926). The scientific linguist *describes* any and all varieties of language without regard to the esteem in which they are held socially.

Some of the work of modern linguists is highly technical. The results of their work are, however, important to scholars in every field. Linguistics is among the most important scientific developments of this century and there has been an explosion in our knowledge of how language works – a 'big bang' which is still continuing and of which this paper is a modest part.

The new knowledge about language has led to a heightened consciousness of the formative role of language in all human activities. Intellectually, it is increasingly clear to scholars in many disciplines, from Theology (Cupitt, 1985)to Economics (McCloskey, 1986), that their knowledge is not merely reflected by language: it is *constituted* by language.

Language is not like plain glass: it is more like glass which is many-coloured, distorted and dirty, and our views on the world are conditioned by its limitations. Language is many-layered: one of the achievements of scientific linguistics is to describe accurately and exhaustively the rules by which the levels combine to make utterances.

All our utterances obey the rules at every level simultaneously. (This is equally true of the spoken language, but speech is even more complicated than writing and we shall restrict our examples to the written language.)

The written language consists of the levels set out on the see chart opposite.

The level of the clause gives a clear example of how our thoughts are both made possible and also limited by the structure of language: every utterance we make has to fall into the pattern of the clause: Subject, Verb, Object – that is, somebody is doing something to somebody or something. (A more technical description of the grammar of the clause is given in Appendix E.) Moreover, each utterance is addressed to a listener or reader, casting him/her into the role of respondent to a statement, question or command. (Halliday, 1973) This rigid structure is obligatory and determines not only what we can *say* but also what we can *think*. This structure applies to all languages – it is clearly innate. (Chomsky, 1968)

At the same time language is infinitely variable. Take, for example, the level of the word – words are constantly entering any language, disappearing

Level	**rules of combination**	**example**
text		7.50 The National Lottery Live Presented by Dale Winton, including more predictions from Mystic Meg. Producer Peter Estall Stereo 667185
↑	discourse analysis	NOTE: winning numbers from previous lottery draws are available on Ceefax page 750 or by calling the Players' Lottery Helpline on 0645 100000
sentences		NOTE: winning numbers from previous lottery draws are available on Ceefax page 750 or by calling the Players' Lottery Helpline on 0645 100000
↑	grammar	
clauses		numbers from previous lottery draws are available on Ceefax page 750
↑	grammar	
words		available
↑	morphology	
morphemes		-able
↑	spelling	
letters		a – b – l – e

from it and changing their meanings as people use them to give shape to new experiences.

It is this structured yet infinitely variable medium in which our cognitive grasp of the world is constituted. Language enables us, as human beings, to create collectively an ever-changing series of patterns which describe our world and enable us to operate within it. Very little in human life is natural: most of it is culturally conditioned by our use of language.

It is the purpose of this paper to show how this comparatively new science can throw light on the particular language variety through which educational discourse across the curriculum is constituted. We shall use the term 'Academic English' to name this variety. (It is sometimes referred to as 'English for Academic Purposes' – Johns, 1996.)

Applied Linguistics

The narrow definition of Applied Linguistics is the field of Teaching English as a Foreign Language (TEFL). The reason for TEFL appropriating to itself the title of Applied Linguistics is that it was the first to seize upon the new insights of scientific Linguistics and apply them.

As recently as thirty years ago a few people were doing an amateurish best to teach English to foreigners in scattered outposts all over the world. Since then there has been a transformation of this field in response to the world-wide demand to learn the international language for a multitude of different purposes. TEFL is now a multi-billion pound industry, highly professional, highly organised, producing an almost embarrassing abundance of commercial teaching materials. TEFL teachers are supported by an army of researchers doing such skilful and professional tasks as needs analysis, syllabus design, testing, teaching methods and teacher training.

A broader definition of Applied Linguistics must include the ever-expanding number of activities which look to Linguistics to solve their problems. For instance, business has realised to the usefulness of employing linguists to improve their communications. Linguists are employed to analyse reports, forms, manuals and correspondence, to suggest linguistic options for rewriting them and to train staff to use them. Recently, one of the authors of this paper spent an hour redesigning a direct debit form: she was paid £50 and the firm made £10,000 in the first fortnight. In this field too Linguistics is big business!

A more sensational aspect of Applied Linguistics is that of Forensic Linguistics (Gibbons, 1994). Leaders in this field are Malcolm Coulthard and his colleagues at the University of Birmingham, where the international journal *Forensic Linguistics* is edited. Using their databanks which show how language is actually used by different people in different situations, forensic linguists are now able to advise on the authenticity of evidence. Most famously, partly as a result of linguistic evidence, the West Midlands Serious Crime Squad was disbanded and the 'Birmingham Six' released.

An area in which linguistics has an expected and natural part to play is the study of literature. Deconstruction, the revolution in literary theory, follows from the understanding that literature, in common with most human activities, is constituted by human language. Stylistics, the bringing of linguistic insights to bear on literature, used to be confined to the analysis of traditional high literature. Critical Discourse Analysis is now extending techniques of stylistic analysis into the politically important – and sensitive – area of media studies (Fairclough, 1989; Toolan, forthcoming).

Language and Education

An area which has so far proved resistant to the insights of Linguistics is mainstream education in this country. Yet the potential of Linguistics for transforming this field is as great as any other area of Applied Linguistics: academic education from school onwards is constituted by natural language. It is therefore accessible to the illuminations of Linguistics, which has the potential to solve some of the most intractable problems of learning across the curriculum.

Here it is instructive to draw a parallel with genetic engineering. People have long been at the mercy of hereditary diseases, but until the theoretical breakthrough which describes the 'language' system of DNA molecules, they were helpless in the face of them. However, as a result of this theoretical breakthrough, Genetic Engineering can now be applied to the prevention and cure of such diseases. In the same way scientific Linguistics can enable us to 'cure' some of the most disabling educational deficiencies.

Teachers have for a long time been intuitively aware that language and education are intimately linked. As long ago as 1959 Basil Bernstein attempted to put this intuition onto a more scientific basis, hypothesising that young people who failed in the education system had a language 'deficit' (Bernstein, 1959). Unfortunately, linguists failed to substantiate Bernstein's hypothesis because the theoretical foundation for a description of academic language was not available at that time. Linguistics in the sixties was limited to working out a scientific system for the description of the grammar of the clause. The linguistic features which were applied to Bernstein's data – for example, expressions of cause – proved to be invalid and Bernstein's work was condemned as illiberal in its suggestion that working-class language was in any way inadequate. (Labov, 1972).

Money was made available in the sixties for producing linguistic materials for use in secondary schools (Doughty *et al*, 1971), but, popular and interesting as these were, they did not address the problem of language across the curriculum. This was a source of some experiment in the seventies and eighties, but fizzled out as, once again, it failed to produce results in terms of widening the access to academic success.

Meanwhile, English teachers had rightly rejected the prescriptive Latin-based model of grammar taught to earlier generations in Grammar Schools, and the formal study of language disappeared from the curriculum. A whole generation of English teachers passed through colleges and universities with no formal language training. Ironically, this was at a time of enormous developments in the scientific understanding of how language works.

The shake-up in education caused by the introduction of the National Curriculum has led to some explicit language study being forced upon reluctant English Departments in schools. The Kingman and Cox Reports (Department of Education and Science, 1988 and 1989) have been used as the basis for the introduction of explicit language teaching, but the development of materials to assist English teachers who themselves know little about language has been slotted into the predominantly literary and humanitarian paradigm of conventional English teaching (HMSO, 1991).

With hindsight we can see that the reason for these failures was the lack of a description of the relevant features of academic language.

The Wigan Language Project

This description is now available and has already been mediated into secondary schools through the Wigan Language Project. A full account of this Project can be found in Mason, Mason and Quayle, 1992.

The Wigan Language Project is so called because it was trialled systematically from 1983 to 1991 at Shevington High School, Wigan, where Bob Mason was Headteacher. Other Wigan secondary schools participated in a number of ways. The Project was supported, morally and financially, by the Metropolitan Borough of Wigan during this period, particularly by seconding Brian Heap to evaluate the Project (Heap, 1988 and 1989).

The first textbooks containing the material of the Project were published by T.R.A.C.E. in Wigan under the title *Illuminating English.* The second edition of these books, which include the theoretical development described in this paper, are being published by Wigan and Leigh College under the new title *Breakthrough to Learning.*

The account below describes:

1. The linguistic theory on which the Project was based

2. The methods of Applied Linguistics, which have been transferred to mainstream teaching.

3. The results in terms of GCSE.

The Wigan Language Project: The Linguistic Theory

There are a number of different linguistic schools. The model used throughout this paper is derived from Systemics. (Halliday, 1984)

The new insights from linguistics which are mediated into schools by *Breakthrough to Learning* are:

(1) Concrete and abstract language

The Wigan Language Project was based on Mary Mason's earlier analysis of the difference between concrete everyday language and abstract academic language at the level of the word. The analysis has been published in Mason, 1986 and 1987.

A further example is included here. The difference between the everyday language which we all share and the Academic English used by the educated and powerful is illustrated by the two texts which follow: They are newspaper articles which appeared on the same day (13/3/95) and were triggered by the same news item – Text A is from *The Daily Mirror* and Text B from *The Guardian.*

The first part of each text (174 words from Text A and 168 from Text B) are analysed in Appendix A, using the model of concrete and abstract language adopted in the Wigan Language Project.

TEXT A *The Mirror* (13/3/95)

Page 1

By BRIAN READE and CAROL MIDGLEY

THE father of cancer girl Little B told last night of the heart-breaking moment when she heard about her own case on the radio.

The 10-year-old leukaemia victim did not know SHE was the unnamed youngster denied treatment by the National Health Service.

174 words

Brave

But her heart went out to the girl in the news report. She told her tearful dad: "I think they should give her the operation."

Today the Daily Mirror launches the 'B' Appeal for leukaemia research — and brave Little B begins her last battle for life. She has only a slim chance.

But her father told the Mirror: "I believe she can pull through."

How YOU can help
SEE PAGE 2

Page 2

How YOU can help

DAILY Mirror 'B' APPEAL

THE Daily Mirror today launches The B Appeal, named after the brave ten-year-old battling against leukaemia whom Harley Street consultant Dr Peter Gravett insisted in the Mirror on Saturday could be successfully treated.

The appeal is to raise cash for research into the potentially killer disease which affects boys and girls such as little B.

The Mirror has donated £10,000 to kick-start the fund, which has the full backing of the girl's father. Now here's your chance to make a contribution. It could not be easier.

Simply go into any of Lloyds Bank's 1,700 branches and pay either cash or by cheque direct into The B Appeal.

Cheques should be made payable to "The B Appeal".

Alternatively you can pledge a credit card donation over the phone from 8am today.

Call The B Appeal donation line on freephone 0800 666-817.

A recorded message on the line will tell you exactly how you can make an instant donation.

For those readers who do not have a local branch of Lloyds Bank, we will be publishing in tomorrow's paper a special donation PO Box number where you can send postal payments.

THE HOTLINE
0800 666-817

TEXT B *The Guardian* (13/3/95)

'Name procedures we cannot afford'

David Brindle

THE National Health Service should decide which types of treatment cannot be afforded from public funds, Sir Douglas Black, former chief scientist at the Department of Health, says today.

Britain should follow the lead of the American state of Oregon which has declared that more than one in six medical procedures will not be available at public cost, Sir Douglas says.

168 words

His comments, in an article criticising the Government's NHS market polices, show that argument over the case for explicit health care rationing spans the spectrum of political and medical opinion.

Ministers have resisted pressure to "do an Oregon". They say decisions must be left to doctors at local level, as in the current case of the 10-year-old leukaemia sufferer denied further treatment by Cambridge health authority.

Sir Douglas says the rationing issue needs to be addressed because demand for health care is being driven by the ageing population, the links between high unemployment and ill-health, and the increasing scope and sophistication of available treatments.

"Exaggerated claims for 'breakthroughs' in treatment have combined with organised consumerism to raise expectations beyond what is realistic on finite resources," he writes.

Rationing by the market is unacceptable. "I further believe that rationing should fall, not on types of service, still less on categories of patients, but on procedures, using the term broadly to include medical and surgical regimens of treatment and measures of prevention."

In Oregon, 688 treatments were ranked by priority, and the 120 "least economic" were excluded from state funding, in an attempt to make the state's limited health care system more effective.

Urging consideration of a similar approach, Sir Douglas says: "It will not be at all easy or rapid to establish a calculus of merit in procedures for health care, but it could be worth doing."

Sir Douglas makes his comments in a foreword to a report claiming the NHS market has diverted at least £1.7 billion a year from patient care into increased bureaucracy.

The report has been drawn up by the Health Policy Network, a group of experts from a variety of backgrounds, set up by the NHS Consultants' Association and backed by the NHS Support Federation, a pressure group.

It says administrative and management overheads of the NHS have doubled to 11.6 per cent of its budget since preparations for the market began in 1991. Doctors and nurses are also spending more time on uncosted extra paperwork.

In Practice: The NHS Market; NHS Consultants' Association, Hill House, Great Bourton, Banbury OX17 1QH; £3.50

Summary
Linguistic features of abstract language

	Text A (174 words)	Text B (168 words)
Latin roots	23	48
Greek roots	2	4
Nominalisations	16	36
Metaphor	6	9
Personification	6	5
Total	53	102

Several points must be made on the basis of this summary:

(1) The same features occur in both texts. Academic language does not have a monopoly of any linguistic features.

(2) However, a simple count of abstract features shows that Text B is very much more abstract than Text A. These features, together with such well-known features of Academic English as the passive voice and complex sentences, are explicitly taught in the Wigan Language Project.

(3) Particularly significant is the greater number of nominalisations in Text B. At the time when the materials used in the Wigan Language Project were being developed, we knew that nominalisation was obviously important and had to form part of the syllabus. The functional significance of nominalisation is a recent insight and will be made explicit later.

Discourse analysis:
This is the description of the way language is organised above the level of the sentence. It shows the underlying structures which govern the way in which sentences combine to form texts. The model used is fully written up elsewhere (Hoey, 1983). It forms the theoretical base for Book 3 of *Breakthrough to Learning: Writing for Learning.*

The Work of the Applied Linguist

The syllabus design and teaching methods used in the Wigan Language Project are those familiar from Applied Linguistics (Teaching English as a Foreign Language). A brief description of the work of the Applied Linguist in this narrow sense follows:

How we learn language(s)

First, it must be said that there are many ways of learning a language. The traditional one, used in multi-lingual communities from time immemorial, is to join the community speaking that language and pick it up by trial and error. In TEFL this lengthy and uncertain way of learning a language has been replaced by a scientific and professional approach made possible by the work of Applied Linguists over several decades.

The method of the Applied Linguist

This is what Applied Linguists do when asked to devise a programme for teaching English to a learner (or group of learners):

First, they use their understanding of the levels of language briefly described above to analyse the following:

(1) Analyses

A. What English does the learner already know?

It is easier to teach learners from scratch than to replace the inaccurate and muddled English that many learners come with. (Such learners are known in the trade as 'false beginners'.) Their particular confusions have to be cleared up.

B. What are the particular problems of transferring from the learner's native language to English?

From the point of view of words and grammar, there is obviously less of a gap between English and French than between English and Chinese. Experience show the kinds of problems that particular language users have in learning English. Howard Jackson did a pioneering analysis of the difficulties likely to be encountered by bilingual pupils in this country in moving from Punjabi to English. (Jackson, 1982)

C. What kind of English does the learner need? (the target language)

Many learners have a limited amount of time in which to learn the kind of English they need for professional purposes, so it is the job of the Applied Linguist to devise a course directed to the style of language each learner needs. The language needed by a pilot is not the same as that needed by a waiter: both are restricted varieties of English, but whereas the waiter's popularity may be enhanced by a picturesque pronunciation, unacceptable pronunciation by a pilot has been a cause of air disasters.

Both pilots and waiters need primarily the spoken language, whereas a scientist may well need only a reading knowledge of English in order to keep up with papers in his field. The applied linguist analyses the variety of English needed by particular learners with all the frameworks at his/her disposal – for example, vocabulary, grammar, discourse structures and skills (listening, speaking, reading writing) etc.

(2) Syllabus

Having carried out the analyses, the Applied Linguist then devises a syllabus to take learners stage by stage from where they are to where they need to go. This may be based on structural (grammatical) or functional principles, or, more recently, on the vocabulary drawn from the huge Cobuild database. (Willis, 1990)

(3) Method

Many fascinating and innovative methods of learning English have been pioneered in the last thirty years. However, the bulk of textbooks remain fairly traditional: the point to be taught is outlined, it is practised formally and then used in context. For example, if a group of words is to be taught, this aim will be stated. Then the learners will practise the pronunciation and/or spelling of the words (the form) and, finally, will practise how they are used in real language (the function).

Applied Linguistics in the Wigan Language Project

How we learn language(s)

Until now, learners in mainstream education have been left, in the absence of an adequate theory, to pick up by trial and error the academic language which is vital for success in school.

This obviously gives a huge advantage to the children of educated people, who are surrounded from their earliest years with the language of education.

It has led to a confusion between the hardware and the software of individual learners. The hardware is the capacity of the individual brain as a computer. No-one has found a culture-free way of measuring this. The software is the educational (i.e. the language) programme which enables the user to bring the power of abstract language to bear upon any subject of study.

It has been the basis of our education system that people succeed because their hardware is superior i.e. they are clever. To make available the educational software (i.e. the language of education) to all is to question that assumption and the selective and socially divisive institutions that are built on it.

The Wigan Language Project is based on the belief that what can be described can be taught. The theoretical description outlined above makes it possible to bring to mainstream education the same professionalism that teachers of English as a Foreign Language have at their disposal.

(1) Analyses

A. What English does the learner already know?
All native speakers of English come to school with a mastery of the spoken concrete language which they need in order to create and maintain their roles in their families and communities. Many non-native speakers have to learn this kind of English at school.

Both native and non-native speakers of English have to learn to read and write sufficiently well to join the community of the educated.

B. What are the particular problems of transferring from the language the learner knows to the target language?
The answer to this question is: very few.

The grammar, pronunciation, spelling and much of the vocabulary of everyday English and academic English are the same. It is much easier to teach learners a different variety of the language they already know than to teach them a foreign language.

C. What kind of English does the learner need?
The target language is Academic English.

(2) Syllabus
The syllabus is constituted by systematically working through those features of academic language which are different from the features of everyday language.

The syllabus of the three books of *Illuminating English* is as follows:

Book 1 *Language Awareness:*

Grammar of the clause: Subject, Verb, Object (English compared with eight other languages from across the world)

Parts of speech (word classes): noun, verb, adjective, adverb, preposition, prefix, particle, pronoun, interjection (English compared with other languages)

Latin and Greek roots

Varieties of English: spoken and written, dialect, pidgin and creole

Book 2 *Reading for Learning:*

Latin and Greek roots

Active and passive voice

Nominalisation

Metaphor and personification

Complex sentences

Book 3 *Writing for Learning*

Problem – solution	
General – particular	in narrative and
Compare – contrast	non-narrative texts
Point of view	

(3) Method

This is the traditional one of (1) stating what is to be taught (2) practising the point formally and (3) practising it in context. Appendix B gives an example.

Distance learning

Because few teachers have any training in Linguistics – and indeed many teachers were, during the trials, hostile to it – the methods of distance learning were used, so giving the learners direct access to the materials. It is suggested that the learners are encouraged to work in pairs, so giving them the opportunity to talk through any difficulties and disagreements. It frees the teacher from preparation and marking – there is nothing which cannot be corrected in class time – and leaves her free to help and encourage individuals.

It is very much in keeping with the modern move to independent learning.

RESULTS

These are written up in Mason, Mason and Quayle (1992) and brought up to date in Mason (1995).

Briefly, Books 1, 2, and 3 were studied by pupils in the 7th, 8th and 9th years respectively from 1984 to 1991. The results came through in a dramatic increase in the percentage of pupils gaining 5 or more GCSEs, grades A – C.

In 1989, when the cohort sitting GCSE had done Book 1, the results were slightly less than the national average – 30% and 33% respectively.

In 1990 the cohort doing GCSE had done Books 1 and 2, and the results shot up to 47%, while the national results rose to only 34%. The following year (1991) the pupils had done all three books of the course. The results rose again to 56%, leaving the national percentage far behind at 36%.

A fuller account is given in Appendix C.

Working with bilingual learners

All the pupils who took part in the Wigan Language Project were native speakers of English.

It is clear, however, that most of the bilingual pupils in our schools will have a deficit in the language of learning similar to that of many working-class native speakers. The exceptions are those who have been through secondary education in another country and so have learned to handle abstract language in their first language. For them it is merely a matter of translating from their first language into English.

Most bilingual pupils in our schools, like most native speakers, depend on school to give them the cognitive development which comes with the mastery of abstract language. It is clear, then, that they stand to gain at least as much as native speakers from *Breakthrough to Learning.* Indeed, bilingual pupils have a twofold advantage over native speakers: first, they are aware of language in a way that only bilingual people can be, and second – and more important – they know that their problems in education come from their incomplete mastery of English. They have not been educationally and socially disabled, in the way that so many native speakers are, by being given the impression that they fail because they are stupid. The old unspoken structure of our schools has been that educational failure is due to the defective hardware of individual pupils, rather than the failure of the schools to insert the appropriate software.

BORDESLEY GREEN GIRLS' SCHOOL, BIRMINGHAM

Programme

An opportunity to use *Breakthrough to Learning* with bilingual pupils arose when in 1993 Joan Sandland, the Head of this 98% bilingual Muslim secondary school, asked Mary Mason, as an Applied Linguist, to draw up a language programme for the school.

Briefly, this was done using the methods described above. For a full account of this see Mason 1994. As a result, space was made on the main timetable for the three books of *Breakthrough to Learning* and also an existing programme of reading improvement was extended.

In addition, a pilot class of tenth year pupils met for an hour a week after school for about nine months to work through a very short version of Books 1 and 2 of *Breakthrough to Learning.* These pupils took GCSE in 1995.

A full account of this work can be found in Mason 1994.

Results

The GCSE results of the pilot group compared with their peers were not available, when the above article went to press.

Briefly, the girls who had taken part in the pilot course gained 1 more GCSE pass, grades A – C, than the pupils who had not taken part.

Details of the results are given in Appendix D.

From Form to Function: the development of the theory

THE QUESTION: WHY ARE NOMINALISATIONS SO CRUCIAL TO ACADEMIC ENGLISH?

We were always conscious that the theoretical foundation of the Wigan Language Project was incomplete. What we had elicited and taught were merely the *formal* features of academic language. And, although the results in terms of academic success were gratifying, we always knew that this was merely the beginning.

It was as though we were analysing the language of story-telling and had spotted a lot of verbs ending in *-ed* (a *formal* feature), without understanding that this signals the past tense (the *function* of this formal feature). Or, as though in examining the language of advertising, we had noted that a lot of adjectives end in *-est* without grasping that this signals the superlative.

It was unsatisfying that we were unable to explain the role of nominalisation in academic language. It was overwhelmingly the most significant feature in school textbooks across the curriculum, as it is in *The Guardian* article (Text B) above. It was clear to us that the nominalisation of verbs is necessary to describe processes (such as *treatment, procedures, rationing* in Text B) and that the nominalisation of adjectives gives us the power to talk about qualities (*kindness, competence, probity* etc.) and conditions (*heat, length, altitude* etc).

We felt that there was more to it than that, and indeed, when we put together the cognitive framework of Geography as an academic subject with the linguistic form of the key words in that subject, we had a very exciting solution to the question.

THE ANSWER

The answer turned out to be amazingly simple. All pupils and teachers who successfully handle academic language have intuitively internalised how it functions. This – as far as we know – is the first time it has been made explicit.

To demonstrate the answer we shall turn back to the extracts from *The Mirror* and *Guardian* (Texts A and B) and apply to them linguistic models.

The one which most powerfully elicits the function of nominalisations is Halliday's transitivity system. An analysis of Texts A and B is given in Appendix E.

Discourse analysis

Here we shall use two elements of discourse analysis (Hoey, 1983) – part of the model used in Book 3 of *Breakthrough to Learning*.

(1) Problem – Solution

Both texts are organised as Situation – Problem – Solution – Outcome.

Text A:
Situation: Little B has leukaemia.
Problem: The NHS refuses further treatment.
Solution: The Daily Mirror launches the Little B Appeal for leukaemia research.
Outcome:???

Text B:
Situation: increasing demand for health care
Problem: finite resources
Solution: rationing
Outcome: ???

Note that it is in the nature of both texts to be unresolved – the outcome is not known. One has to buy further newspapers to discover what happens next.

(2) **General – Particular**

The role of Little B reveals one of the most significant differences between these texts:

In *The Guardian* her case is referred to as merely as a particular example of the general problem being considered by the article – *as in the current case of the ten-year-old leukaemia sufferer denied further treatment by the Cambridge Health Authority.*

The Mirror item, by contrast, is entirely focussed on the particular plight of Little B. She is the agent of ten of the verbs in the text and her father the agent of two more. The text is almost entirely concerned with the particulars of her case.

Stories and Systems

Everyday language – stories

Stories are the way in which human beings make sense of the everyday world. A story is a series of events linked in time sequence and based on the Problem – Solution pattern. Stories belong to the world of concrete everyday events. These events are fixed by virtue of being in the past.

Text A (*The Mirror*)is a story. The agents are people, institutions with which everyone is familiar, and a personified evil (disease).

The story is about the experience of particular people. There are more verbs of Mental Process than any other kind: two express feelings (*heart-breaking, her heart went out*), one perceiving (*heard*), three cognition (*did not know, think, believe*) and five telling (*told – 3 times), report, insisted*).

The solution which *The Mirror* offers is no solution at all to the particular problem of Little B. A later development of the 'story' told of an anonymous donor who paid for the private treatment of the child, giving her a few more months of life. *The Mirror's* 'solution' can do no more than make readers feel they can do something concrete by giving money.

The Mirror's readers will buy future papers to discover how the story ends – sadly, some months later with the death of Little B.

Academic language – variables

Text B (*The Guardian*) is not a story. The agents in Text B are not people but ideas or concepts.

These ideas are made possible by the option which exists within the language system of nominalisation – changing verbs and adjectives into nouns. For example: the verb *to treat* can be made into the noun *treatment* by adding the suffix – *ment.*

We shall examine the clause: *demand for health care is being driven by the ageing population, the links between high unemployment and ill-health, and the increasing scope and sophistication of available treatments,* starting with the word *unemployment.*

Nominalisation sets the verb free from the particular. A verb has a subject and may have an object (*The firm employs my mother.*) By nominalising the verb *employ* we have a concept – *employment.* This is now a noun and so can be made negative – unemployment. It can also be qualified by an adjective – *high.* Most importantly, it can be related to another concept – *ill-health.* In this case it is done by using the metaphor *link* – *the links between high unemployment and ill-health.* These concepts join further nominalisations – *the ageing population and the increasing scope and sophistication of available treatments* to act together as the agent in the passive sentence: *demand for health care is being driven by ....*

All these nominalisations are variables. They vary in that they are not limited by particular subjects and objects, nor by time and space.

This answers the question that had troubled us for so long: why are academic texts so full of nominalisations? The answer is that they make it possible to think in terms of variables.

What people are doing when they use this kind of language is try out patterns of variables until they arrive at some kind of system. In the case of Text B the tentativeness of any such system can be seen. No solution is going to be either satisfactory or permanent (though it may be presented as such to the public).

The outcome, which readers will look out for in future papers, is the decision which will be made on the basis of discussions such as these. But any outcome will constitute a further problem – if rationing is adopted and becomes the new *Situation*, there will be many new problems to consider. Texts such as these, in contrast with *The Mirror's* story of Little B, can never have a definite ending.

This description shows how three characteristics of academic language are embodied in particular linguistic forms:

(1) Impersonality

The only named person in Text B is there by virtue of his expert opinion on the subject. The participants in this text are ideas and the institutions which may eventually put these ideas into practice. There are only two verbs of Mental Process and they are of cognition – *show, opinion.*

Another feature of nominalisation is part of the impersonality of the text: a verb has a subject and may have an object. A nominalisation need have neither. In the text many of the nominalisations have no agent – for example, *argument, rationing, pressure, unemployment.*

The impersonality of academic writing is seen also in the use of the passive voice without the agent – for example, *decisions must be left to doctors at local level* (by whom?); *the rationing issue needs to be addressed* (by whom?); *In Oregon, 688 treatments were ranked by priority* (by whom?). This device can be used to avoid responsibility, but it also leaves the participants in the discussion free to consider a possible process without having to decide immediately who may be responsible for carrying it out.

(2) The free play of ideas

All kinds of ideas are put into play and all kinds of solutions are open for discussion. Each of the elements in the Problem – Solution analysis above is elaborated by further ideas in the second part of the text. It may be summarised as follows:

Situation:

organised consumerism

unemployment
(links with ill-health)

ageing population

INCREASING DEMAND FOR HEALTH CARE

raised expectations

'breakthroughs' in treatment

scope and sophistication of treatments

Problem:

FINITE RESOURCES

diverted into bureaucracy

Solution:

by the market

by types of service

RATIONING

by categories of patient

by procedures (as in Oregon)

The ideas put forward here do not claim to be exhaustive. People engaged in discussions on the subject are free to add further ideas.

Another linguistic feature of texts like this is the heavy clustering of nominalisations into very long nominal groups – as in the example given above.

(3) The language of power

On the basis of such discussions and articles in language like this, decisions will be made which will affect the lives of everybody – including future Little Bs.

Contrast the irrelevance of *The Mirror's* 'solution' – the story is told for people who have no expectations of exercising real power over the lives of other people – or, indeed, their own.

Variables and Systems: an example from Geography

The point will be illustrated by examining in more detail the derivation and possible use of the word *erosion*:

Erosion: This abstract word is formed (like all other abstract words) from a concrete root: in this case, from Latin *rodere* – to gnaw. To describe the effects of wind and water on the physical landscape, *wind* and *water* have to be personified: they *gnaw* at the landscape, as a person (or other animate being) gnaws at a bone.

Another verb for describing erosion is to *wear away* – an alternative personification. It is impossible to express this concept in non-metaphorical terms. Like all personifications it ascribes intentionality to entities – *wind* and *water* which, unlike human beings, are not capable of intention. Personification is a branch of metaphor very commonly found in academic texts.

As so often, the technical word selected – *erode* – derives from Latin, for so many centuries the language of ideas throughout Europe. Thus in English there is no derivational link between the concrete word *gnaw* and the abstract word *erode*. German *zerfressen – to erode*, for example, is clearly derived from *fressen – to eat.* (See Mason, 1986 and 1987)

Thus personification produces a verb *erode*, which expresses the action of wind and water on the landscape. This enables us to generate a very large number of sentences, descriptive of this process. For example:

SUBJECT	VERB	OBJECT
wind		
		rocks
ice		shorelines
rain		river beds
water — rivers	*erode*	glacier beds
seas		soil
chemicals		buildings

So long as *erode* remains a verb, it can express only a particular example of the action of eroding agents on the landscape.

If we want to generalise, we have to change the verb *erode* into the abstract noun *erosion*. In doing so, we shed the subjects, *wind, water* etc. and the objects; *rocks, shorelines* etc.

This has the effect of reducing a **clause**, or rather a large number of potential clauses, to a **word**. This makes it available for being operated on **again** at the level of the clause. Thus it can be related to other processes, such as *precipitation, deforestation, vegetation* etc. Any of these can also be related to **properties**, derived by nominalisation from adjectives: for example, *height* or *altitude.*

Using erosion as a variable

The nominalised forms may be used in a variety of ways. The most powerful one, however, is that, as concepts, they are available for use as variables, so creating systems. This is the paradigm of scientific discourse.

Erosion, for example, may be used as a variable in the system of the *landscape.* The choice of variables depends on the purpose of the study.

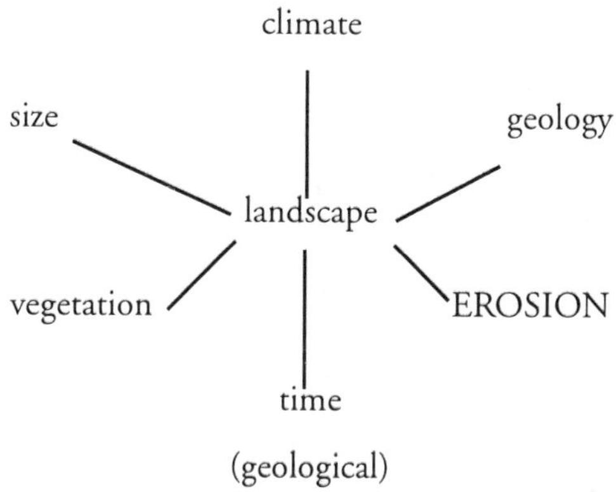

Or *erosion* may be used as a system in itself, to which other concepts relate. For example:

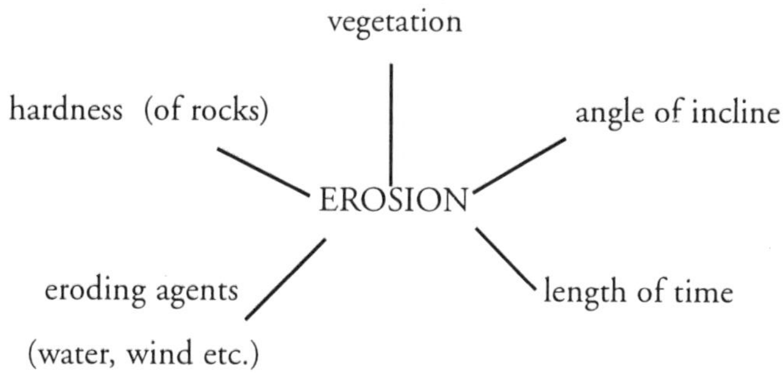

Often it is useful to see the object of study as a series of interlocking systems. The example below gives some of the systems which may be regarded as factors in the central system of *erosion.*

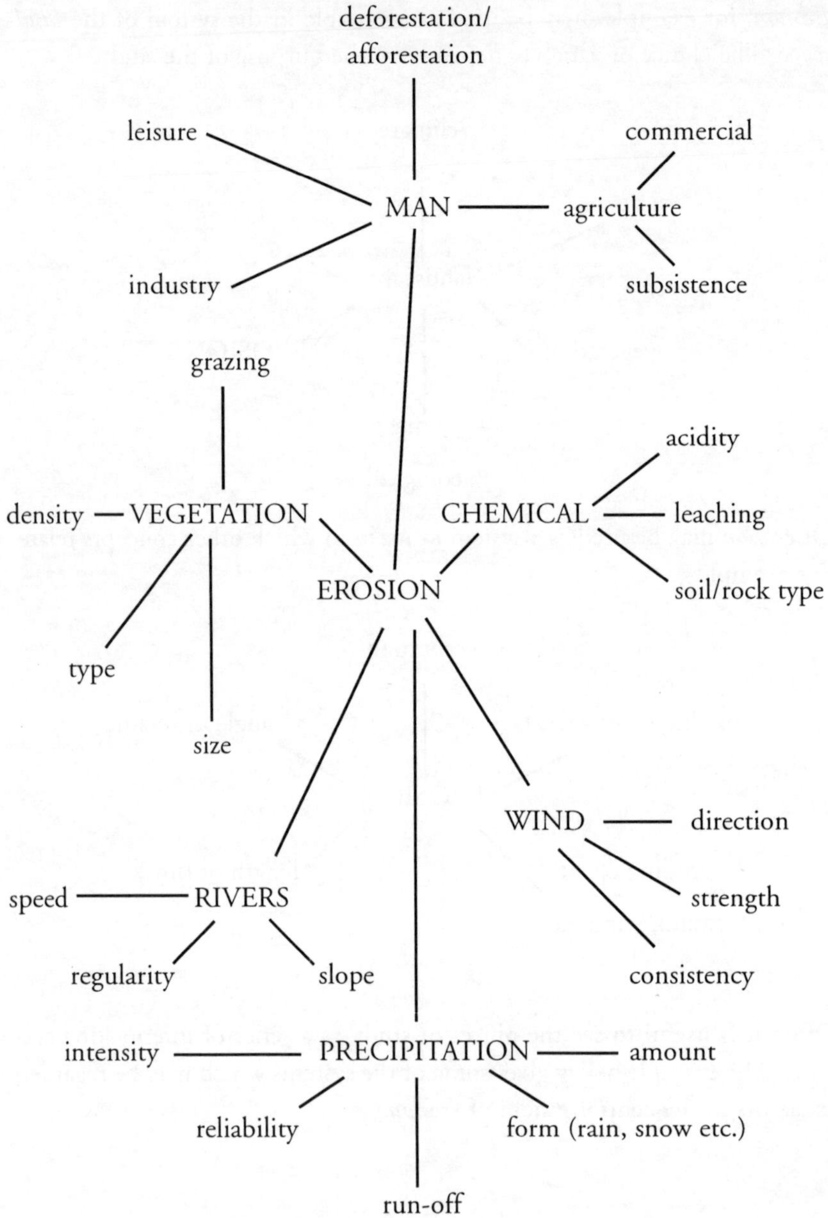
deforestation/
afforestation
leisure
commercial
MAN
agriculture
industry
subsistence
grazing
acidity
density
VEGETATION
CHEMICAL
leaching
EROSION
soil/rock type
type
size
WIND
direction
speed
RIVERS
strength
regularity
slope
consistency
intensity
PRECIPITATION
amount
reliability
form (rain, snow etc.)
run-off

Note that all the variables are nominalisations. There can be no clearer example of the way in which language constitutes thought.

The diagrams above bear an interesting resemblance to the mental maps used by Tony Buzan in his influential book on study skills. (Buzan, 1989)

From these systems of variables (or mental maps), students will compose texts to suit their individual purposes or tasks, using the discourse structures and syntax most appropriate. They will join the ones relevant to their purposes in relationships of cause/effect, question/answer, problem/solution, compare/contrast, advantages/disadvantages, stopping at appropriate moments to give particular examples of their generalisations.

For instance, if they want to consider erosion as a **problem**, they will choose to work with such variables as: *deforestation, over-use of footpaths, cavern and cliff collapse, flooding, hurricanes, monoculture*, using cause/effect and, probably, compare/contrast to make their textual framework. If they choose to examine the positive effects of *erosion*, however, they will select such variables as *deposition for sedimentation for future rocks, valuable agricultural land* and *mineral resources*, perhaps using a question/answer framework. If they decide to study erosion in the tropics, they will select variables such as *amount and intensity of rainfall, humidity, agriculture, leaching, flooding* etc., linking them by, for instance, cause/effect or question/answer frameworks. Another possible study or teaching programme could be erosion in connection with hydro-electric power: the relevant variables will then be: *creation of deep valleys, rainfall, silting of dams, type of rocks* etc. Any or all of the available discourse structures can be used to create an infinite variety of texts.

Systems

The idea of systems relates interestingly to the history of ideas, as expounded, for instance, by Kuhn (1960) and Foucault (1970). Kuhn showed how scientists work in a given framework of ideas (or *paradigm*, as he calls it). This paradigm is taken for granted until it begins to break down under the stress of evidence which does not fit the paradigm. The time is then ripe for a change of paradigm. An example of a paradigm shift in Linguistics is the shift from a diachronic to a synchronic (systemic) approach in the work of De Saussure (1916).

Foucault uses the word *episteme* for this framework of ideas, adding that we are unconscious of the episteme we work within, until it has already changed. It may well be that the dominant episteme (Foucault) or paradigm (Kuhn) of our era is systems of variables.

Language and Mathematics

Educational success depends on more than the mastery of Academic language. The sciences demand that educated people are familiar also with the languages of Mathematics.

Here too nominalisation is the key. Mathematics depends on measurement and the intention to measure something must first be stated in natural language. If one is restricted to concrete language, one is restricted to Arithmetic and the measurement of particular objects. Mathematics depends on the measurement of variables represented by nominalisations such as *height, humidity, pressure, evaporation.*

It is the mathematisation of knowledge which distinguishes the sciences from the arts. Geography, from which the example above was taken, is a subject which has moved from the arts to the sciences in the last half century.

Language Across the Curriculum

We must repeat that the description of academic language given here applies to all subjects across the curriculum. When subjects which were formerly unexamined make a bid to be examined at GCSE they must structure their subject area in terms of variables and systems.

The contents page of a textbook for GCSE in Physical Education called 'Sport Examined' illustrates this point. The words in italics are nominalisations acting as variables in the system of the study of Physical Education.

In Appendix F three passages from school textbooks – Science, Geography and History – are analysed, using the frameworks outlined here. This illustrates the fact that the intellectual framework for all these subjects is essentially the same – only the subject matter is different.

Introduction

PART 1 BODY IN *ACTION*
1 The human body

2 *Food* and *diet*

3 Physical *fitness*

4 *Sport* and *injury*

5 *Measuring* physical *performance*

6 Drugs and *sport*

7 *Success* in *sport*

PART 2 SPORT IN SOCIETY
8 History of *sport*

9 *Amateurism* and *professionalism* in British *sport*

10 *Organisation* of *sport* in Britain at national level

11 *Organisation* of *sport* in Britain at local level

12 *Sponsorship* in *sport*

13 *Sport, entertainment* and the spectator

14 *Leisure* and *sport*

15 *Sport* as a career

16 Women and *sport*

17 International *sport* and *politics*

Index

Paul Beashel and John Taylor: *Sport Examined*, Macmillan 1986

Conclusions

(1) The power of Linguistics

The theory described in this paper illustrates the power of linguistic theory in deconstructing human activities which are constituted by language. In this case the structure of academic texts across the curriculum is made explicit for the first time. It explains what we are doing when we engage in academic discourse. This is quite different from what we are doing when we engage in everyday discourse.

(2) Potential for mainstream education

This has enormous practical implications for mainstream education in this country and, indeed, in any country where the language of education is English. The results of the earlier theory which described the formal features of academic English in the Wigan Language Project were impressive enough. The results of the application of the functional analysis described in this paper must produce an even greater effect.

The revised version of Book 2 of *Breakthrough to Learning* includes these new insights. (Appendix G)

Learners come to school at least as expert as their teachers in the concrete language which they need in order to play a part in their social world. This they – like all of us in this part of our lives – structure as story.

What they find in school is a totally different use of language, one which at least some of their teachers use fluently without being aware of it. Their teachers know intuitively the value of such language, but without being able to explain it, their pupils may well remain mystified by what is going on in school. Teachers and pupils literally do not speak the same language.

At worst, if pupils fail to grasp the purpose of academic work, they may reject it as irrelevant to their own lives. This indifference to school may be exacerbated into hostility if they sense that middle class cultural norms are being imposed, so attempting to break their solidarity with their families and friends.

Experience of even the first stage of the Wigan Language Project suggests that this hostility can be broken if pupils realise that the language of school is the language of power. They can participate in this discourse without changing their cultural norms and allegiances.

(4) The free play of ideas

A mastery of academic language depends on the learner feeling confident enough to make mistakes. Academic thought at its highest level is akin to play: the greatest breakthroughs are made when scholars are trying out ideas for fun.

Freedom to make mistakes is a fundamental feature of learning in general. Yet too many children in our schools still have their confidence sapped by the continual experience of failure. Very young children, enjoying school and freely experimenting in learning, are all too easily turned into alienated and aggressive teenagers, convinced either they are stupid or (sometimes justifiably) that school is stupid.

The method of independent learning adopted in *Breakthrough to Learning* fits this openness of approach. Free from an authority figure who is all too often driven into asserting his/her authority by virtue of superior knowledge, learners are free to make their own errors and judgments and use the information about the language of learning for their own individual purposes and concerns.

There is a place for accuracy, of course. No-one wants to be operated on by a surgeon who knows more about academic discussion than the detail of the human anatomy. But successful surgeons know more than the 'facts' of anatomy – which are themselves subject to individual variation. They operates in conditions which can change rapidly and throw up unexpected dilemmas. There is always an element of uncertainty. The surgeon must act by eliminating some variables and using others as constants.

The tentativeness of knowledge is an essential feature of education. It is especially indispensable in our rapidly changing world. At present it is available only to the minority. The ideas outlined in this paper make it possible to extend it to the majority.

We are all frightened when driving in fog and avoid it when possible. The fog which has hitherto enveloped education has been the language which constitutes it. The application of scientific linguistics to mainstream education can dissipate both the fog and the fear. *Breakthrough to Learning* can give people the confidence to take advantage of learning and to enjoy it at any stage in their lives. (Hellawell, 1995).

APPENDIX A

FORMAL ANALYSIS OF CONCRETE/ABSTRACT LANGUAGE IN TEXTS A AND B

The analysis below is based on **models** of concrete and abstract language. These are theoretical constructs, and any real texts are likely to contain examples of both kinds of language, as do the ones used here.

The first 174 words of Text A and the first 168 words of text B are analysed here in terms of concrete and abstract words.

(1) Concrete language:

It cannot be stressed too strongly that this is the most important part of –language and is mastered in its spoken form by all normal human beings.

'Language originated in and has its primary reference to everyday life; it refers above all to the reality I experience in wide-awake consciousness, which is dominated by the pragmatic motive (that is the cluster of meanings directly pertaining to present or future actions) and which I share with others in a taken-for-granted manner.' (Berger and Luckmann, 1967)

These are the features of concrete language which will be enumerated here:

A. Notional definitions of parts of speech (word-classes)

Nouns, verbs and adjectives can be defined in the terms of traditional Aristotelian grammar: nouns are naming-words, verbs doing-words and adjectives describing-words.

Concrete nouns in Text A:
father, girl, night, radio, dad, little B, the .... ten-year-old, boys, girls

Concrete nouns in Text B:
Sir Douglas Black, Britain, Oregon

C. Literal, not metaphoric.
The concrete nouns above all refer literally to some object which has spatial and temporal dimensions. They are first order nominals (Lyons, 1977)

(2) Abstract language:
Abstract language makes it possible for us to think about **ideas** or **concepts**. The language of ideas is constituted by using extra options within the language system. We shall consider here nominalisation and metaphor.

In English (unlike, for example, German, French, Bulgarian or Spanish) the connection between the concrete word and its abstract derivative is lost, because the former is Anglo-Saxon in origin and the latter Latin or Greek. For example, the concrete word *heal* is Anglo-Saxon and there is no etymological connection between that and *medical*, derived from the Latin *medeor* 'to heal'.

'Most abstract vocabulary was in fact concrete in origin, but this is obscured for speakers of English because abstract terms are typically borrowed from Latin or Greek and we are no longer aware of their original concrete senses: e.g. *despise*, Latin *despicere*, from *de* 'down' and *specere* 'to look'. We become aware of it when the same thing happens with native words, e.g. *look down on*.' (Halliday, 1984)

Latin and Greek roots:

Text A:
Latin: *cancer, case, victim, denied, treatment, National, Service, report, operation, Appeal* (3), *research* (2), *battle, chance, battling, consultant, insisted, treated, successfully, potentially, affects*

Greek: *leukaemia* (2)

Text B:

Latin: *National* (2), *Service* (2), *decide, afforded, public* (2), *funds, scientist, Department, state, declared, medical* (2), *procedures, available* (2), *cost, comments, article, criticising, Government, policies, argument, case* (2), *explicit, rationing* (2), *spectrum, political, opinion, resisted, pressure, decisions, local, level, denied, treatment* (2), *authority, issue, addressed, demand, population, increasing, unemployment*

Greek: *types, scope, sophistication, leukaemia*

A. Nominalisation

Text A:

Abstract nouns made from verbs: *moment, case, treatment, Nation(al), Health, Service, report, operation, research* (2), *battle, life, chance, Appeal* (3)

Concrete nouns from verbs: *consultant, killer*

Concrete nouns from adjectives: *youngster*

Text B:

Abstract nouns made from verbs: *Nation(al)* (2), *Health* (4), *Service* (2), *types, treatment* (3), *funds, Department, state, procedures, cost, Government, argument, case* (2), *rationing* (2), *spectrum, opinion, pressure, decisions, issue, demand, care, population, link, unemployment, scope, sophistication*

Concrete nouns from verbs: *scientist, sufferer, doctors*

Nouns from adjectives: no examples

Abstract noun from concrete noun: *authority*

B. Metaphor:

Text A:

cancer, victim, battle for life, a slim chance, she can pull through, battling

Personification:
(heart-breaking) moment, (denied treatment by) the National Health Service, her heart (went out), The Daily Mirror (launches) (2), *(killer) disease*

Text B:
market, spans the spectrum, resisted pressure, do an Oregon, level, current, issue, links, high (unemployment)

Personification:
Britain should (follow the lead), The National Health Service (should decide), Oregon (has declared), (denied treatment by) Cambridge Health Authority, (being driven by) the ageing population, the links between high unemployment and ill-health etc.

APPENDIX B

BREAKTHROUGH TO LEARNING

BOOK 1
CHAPTER 5

Chapter 5 – **Grammar**

Nouns

In this chapter you will learn:

1 What Grammar is

2 Nouns:

What we do with them
How you can tell a noun from other words
How our choice of noun shows our point of view

3 That all languages have nouns

4 That some languages have a word for 'the' and some do not.

CORE **Chapter 5 –**

1

Introduction: What grammar is

When we describe an instrument, we first label its parts:

For example: **The torch**

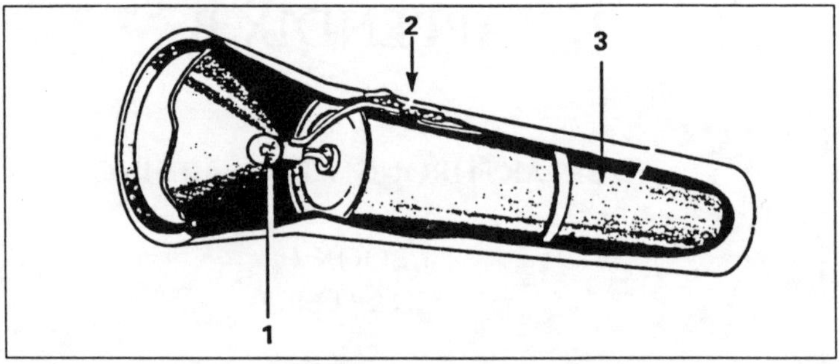

Write on your paper the numbers 1-3.

Write against them the part of the torch that has this number in the diagram.

switch	battery	bulb

These are the parts of the torch.

In our description of the instrument, we then say what each part does.

Match these columns by writing the numbers 1-3 on your paper and A. B or C against each.

Part of the torch	What it does
1. battery	**A.** turns the power on and off.
2. bulb	**B.** supplies electric power.
3. switch	**C.** turns electricity into heat and light.

Because the parts of the torch work together, we are able use the torch for a certain purpose.

Write on your paper the number which describes purpose of the torch:

1. to light a fire **2.** to find our way in the dark **3.** to play a tune.

– Nouns **CORE**

2

Grammar

Human language is a much more complicated and powerful instrument than a torch.

Like a torch it has parts, traditionally called **parts of speech**.

Like the bulb, battery and switch of a torch, each part of speech **does** different things in the sentence and obeys rules different from the other parts of speech.

The sections in this course called **Grammar** describe the parts of speech and what they do in the sentence.

Like a torch, language has a purpose: we use it to communicate with one another and to talk about the world.

Language has made human beings the most powerful creatures on earth: by using it, we co-operate to change the world.

3

Nouns

The first of speech is the **noun**. Our senses tell us that things exist in the world. Nouns enable us to name them.

Write down six nouns that name things in the room you are in now.

For example: *chair, pen, goldfish*

Write down	three things we can hear three things we can touch	three things we can smell three things we can taste

For example: *<u>Hear</u> I. music 2. . . . . . 3. . . . . .*

Put a tick against those we can see as well.

How nouns differ from other parts of speech

Nouns, unlike other parts of speech, can have **the** in front of them.
Note that they do not **always** have **the** in front of them, but they **can** have.

For example: He never sits on chairs. She dislikes **the** chairs.

Chair is a noun for two reasons:

1. It names something in the world. **2.** It can have **the** in front of it.

The technical word for **the** is the **definite article**.

Look through the nouns you have written down.

Check that you can put **the** in front of each one.

CORE **Chapter 5 –**

4 Naming (or labelling)

In all school subjects we name things and their parts, using **nouns**.

In Maths we name the circle and its parts:

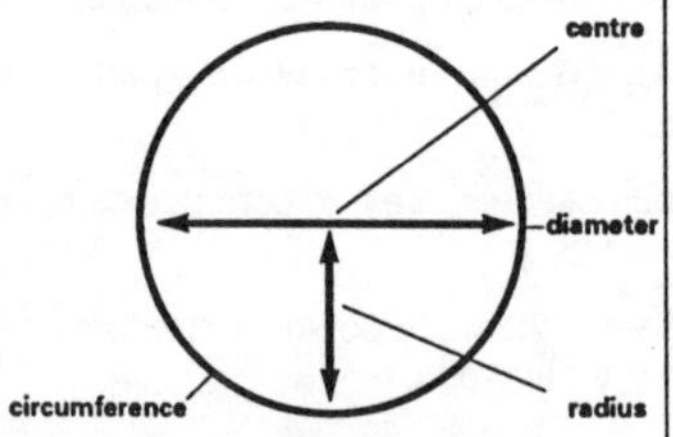

In Physics we name the atom and its parts.

Atom (of hydrogen)

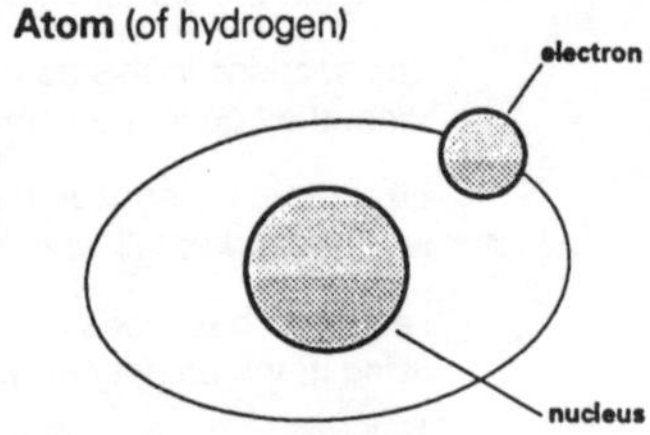

In Botany we name the plant and its parts:.

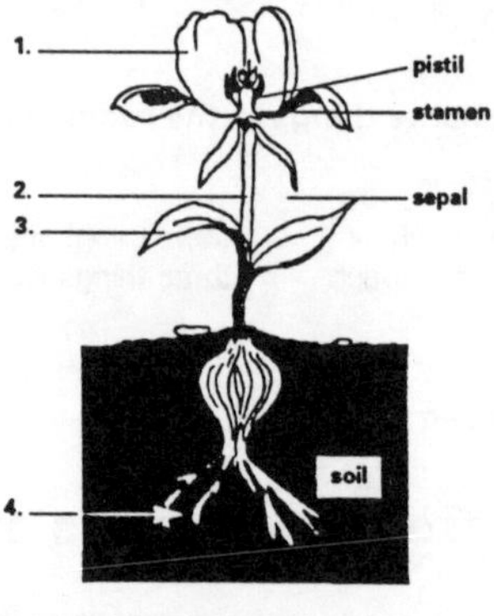

In History we name the medieval castle and its parts:.

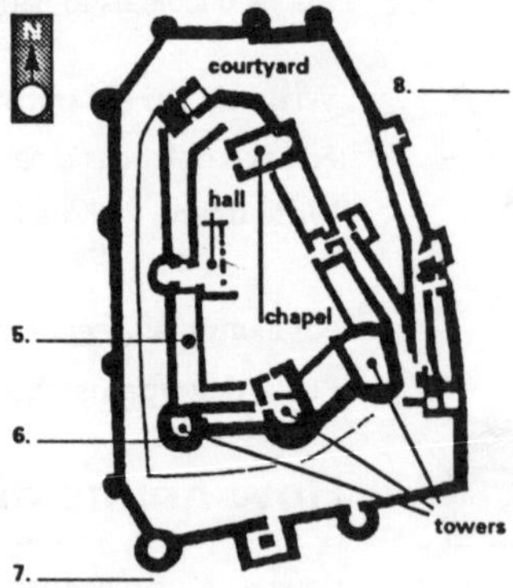

Write 1-4 on your paper.

Write, against the numbers, the nouns for the parts of the plant which are not labelled.

Use these words:

stem	root	petal	leaf

– Nouns **CORE**

Write 5-8 on your paper.

Write, against the numbers, the nouns for the parts of the castle which are not labelled.

Use these words:

south-west tower	south wall	outer gate	well

5

Point of View: Nouns

According to our point of view, we use **different nouns** for the **same things**.

If we like somebody or something, we call them by one noun. If we dislike them, we call them by another.

For example: If someone is playing a record I like, I call it **music**.
Someone who does not like it will call it a **din** or **racket**.

Match the columns below:

For example: *1 C*

We like these	**We dislike these**
1. music	**A.** cur
2. flower	**B.** banger
3. car	**C.** din
4. dog	**D.** brat
5. child	**E.** weed

6

Nouns in 8 languages

Look at the following information about nouns.

Language				Definite Article
***Arabic**	shajara	walad	kalb	al shajara
***Bulgarian**	durvo	dete	kooche	-to, -ut, -ta, -te (durvoto)
***Chinese**	shù	háizi	gou	
English	tree	child	dog	the tree
***Russian**	derevo	rebyonok	sobaka	
***Urdu**	drukht	bucha	koota	
Welsh	coeden	plentyn	ci	yr, y, 'r (y coeden)
Yoruba (Nigeria)	igi	ọmọ	aja	-na (igi na)

*These languages have their own scripts.

Answer these questions:

1. Which languages have no definite article (word for **the**)?
2. Which languages have the definite article before the noun? (English is one of them.)
3. Which languages have the definite article after the noun?
4. In which languages is the definite article always the same?
5. In which languages is the definite article different?
6. Which languages has two words for **child** (according to whether it is under 5 years old or over)?
7. Which languages have a similar word for **tree**?
8. Which languages have a similar word for **dog**?

Add to the table any other language(s) you know.

– Nouns	EXTENSION

7

i

Using your informants

If you are working in class, your teacher will tell you how and when to do this.

If you are working alone, you can make your own arrangements.

Ask your informants these questions about the languages they know:

1. What are the nouns for **child**, **dog**, **tree**?

2. Is there a word for **the**? If so, does it come before or after the noun? Does it change according to the noun it goes with or is it always the same (as in English)?

Note to the teacher: If there are informants in the class, you can do this exercise on the spot. If not, the pupils will have to do it for homework and report back.

8

Recipes

In Cookery we name the things we need to make a dish. That is, we list the ingredients, using nouns. For example: **Scones**

Ingredients: flour	salt	sugar	egg	fat	water	

List the ingredients of your favourite recipe.

9

Plan of your house

Draw a rough plan of your house or flat.

Label the parts - that is, name them, using nouns.

Use some of these words and others if you need them:

kitchen	bedroom	lounge	bathroom
garage	staircase	porch	lavatory
corridor	dining room	conservatory	loft

EXTENSION **Chapter 5**

10

Mouse's eye view

At the beginning of this lesson you wrote down a list of nouns referring to things or people in the classroom. You named the things that seemed important from **your** point of view.

If a mouse appeared in the corner of the classroom, its point of view would be different. If a mouse had language, it would name quite different things from you.

Write down some things that a mouse would name.

For example: *crumbs.*

Game

"I went to market and I bought . . . "

The first player says one thing he bought. The second player repeats the sentence and adds something else. And so on

So the third player might say: "I went to market and I bought some eggs, a book and a packet of cornflakes".

If a player forgets one of the things, he drops out. The winner is the one who is left.

You can ring the changes on this game by playing: "I went to a party and I wore . . . ." or: "I went to a cafe and I ate . . . ."

The words which refer to what you buy (or wear or eat) are nouns.

APPENDIX C

An account of the early informal trials at Shevington High School from 1983 is given in Mason, Mason and Quayle 1992. This article also describes the work of Brian Heap, who was seconded to the University of Lancaster for two years in order to evaluate the Project for the Metropolitan Borough of Wigan.

The formal trials were conducted from 1986 to 1991, when the three books of *Breakthrough to Learning* (now retitled *Illuminating English*) were worked through by all pupils in Years 7-9.

The results came through three years later in dramatically improved GCSE results across the curriculum. The graph shows these results, using the national results and the Wigan results as controls.

In 1990 Bob Mason retired as Headteacher of the school and the new head abandoned the Project. However, the pupils sitting GCSE in 1992 had already done all three parts of the course, those sitting GCSE in 1993 had done Books 1 and 2 and those sitting GCSE in 1994 had done only Book 1.

The graph shows that while the national results and the Wigan results show a steady increase over the period, the Shevington High School results rise and fall with the use of the course, until by 1994, they are once again similar to the national and Wigan results.

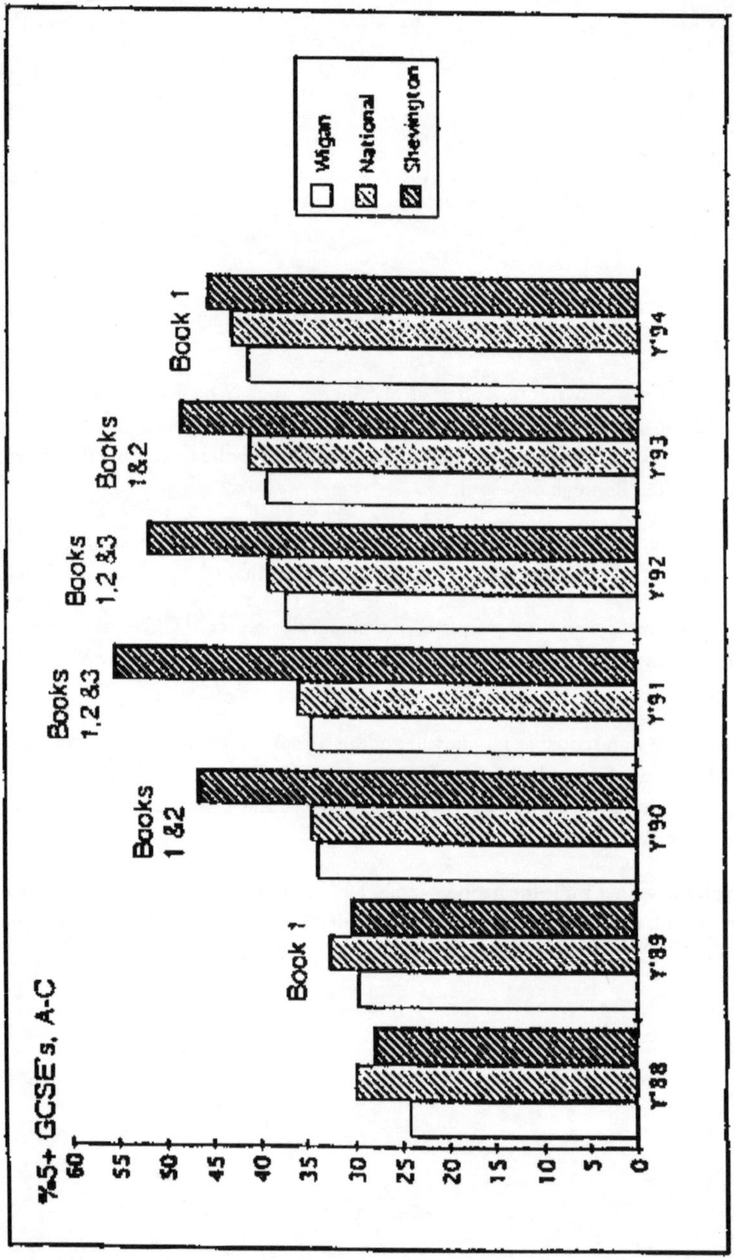
%5+ GCSE's, A-C
60
55
50
45
40
35
30
25
20
15
10
5
0
Y'88
Y'89
Y'90
Y'91
Y'92
Y'93
Y'94
Book 1
Books 1 &2
Books 1,2 &3
Books 1,2 &3
Books 1&2
Book 1
Wigan
National
Shevington

APPENDIX D

BORDESLEY GREEN GIRLS' SCHOOL
PILOT PROGRAMME WITH TENTH YEAR 1993-95

98% of the pupils in this school are bilingual. At the time of the pilot programme the school was banded, with two classes in each band.

The tenth year in 1993 was offered the opportunity of following a shortened version of Books 1 and 2 of *Breakthrough to Learning* in a voluntary class after school once a week for nine months.

The numbers are small and there are other variables, such as the fact that it is likely that some of the girls doing the course were better motivated than the control group, since the class was voluntary.

Nevertheless the GCSE results of this cohort are impressive (see chart).

The school has now made room on its timetable for the three books of the course in years 8-10.

TOP BAND

	average number GCSEs grades A-C	%
Pupils who took course (26)	4.8	46
Pupils who did not (31)	3.3	25

	average number GCSEs grades A-D	%
Pupils who took course (26)	6.5	80
Pupils who did not (31)	5.1	38

BOTTOM BAND

	average number GCSEs grades A-C
Pupils who took course (9)	0.88
Pupils who did not (31)	0.45

	average number GCSEs grades A-D
Pupils who took course (9)	2.33
Pupils who did not (31)	0.72

APPENDIX E

TRANSITIVITY SYSTEM

Halliday's Transitivity System is a semantic analysis of English verbs ('processes'). It is particularly effective in eliciting power relationships. (For example: Burton 1982)

Two changes were made to the system in order to exhaustively analyse Texts A and B:

(1) Some verbs, such as *name, deny, appeal, decide, declare,* fall outside the transitivity system. These are all speech acts (Austen 1962), so this is added as a separate category.

(2) The condition for entering the transitivity system is that of being a clause. However, we decided to add to the clauses the nominalised verbs in the two Texts in order to make a complete analysis of the verbs.

These changes are given in capitals in the model of the transitivity system on page 61.

There are many interesting differences between the two texts – for instance, the kinds of processes and the kinds of participants in those processes. Some of these are referred to in the main text of the paper.

ROLE OF NOMINALISATIONS

What is thrown up very clearly by this analysis is the point most relevant to our argument: in Text A all the participants (or, to use Halliday's earlier term 'agents') are people (*Little B, her father etc.)* or institutions *(the National Health Service, the Mirror* etc.)

In Text B some of the participants are people (*Sir Douglas Black, ministers* etc.) and institutions (*Oregon, Cambridge Health authority* etc.) However, on page 50 the ACTOR in the

PROCESS *is being driven* is not a person or an institution but a series of nominalisations – *the ageing population, the links between high unemployment and ill-health and the increasing scope and sophistication of treatments.*

In other words nominalisations can act as participants Further examples are: *rationing issues, demand for health care, the spectrum of political and medical opinion, the argument over explicit care rationing.*

We are then in a position to ask: what are such nominalisations doing when they are taking on the role of participants? The answer is that they are acting as variables.

TRANSITIVITY SYSTEM (AMENDED)

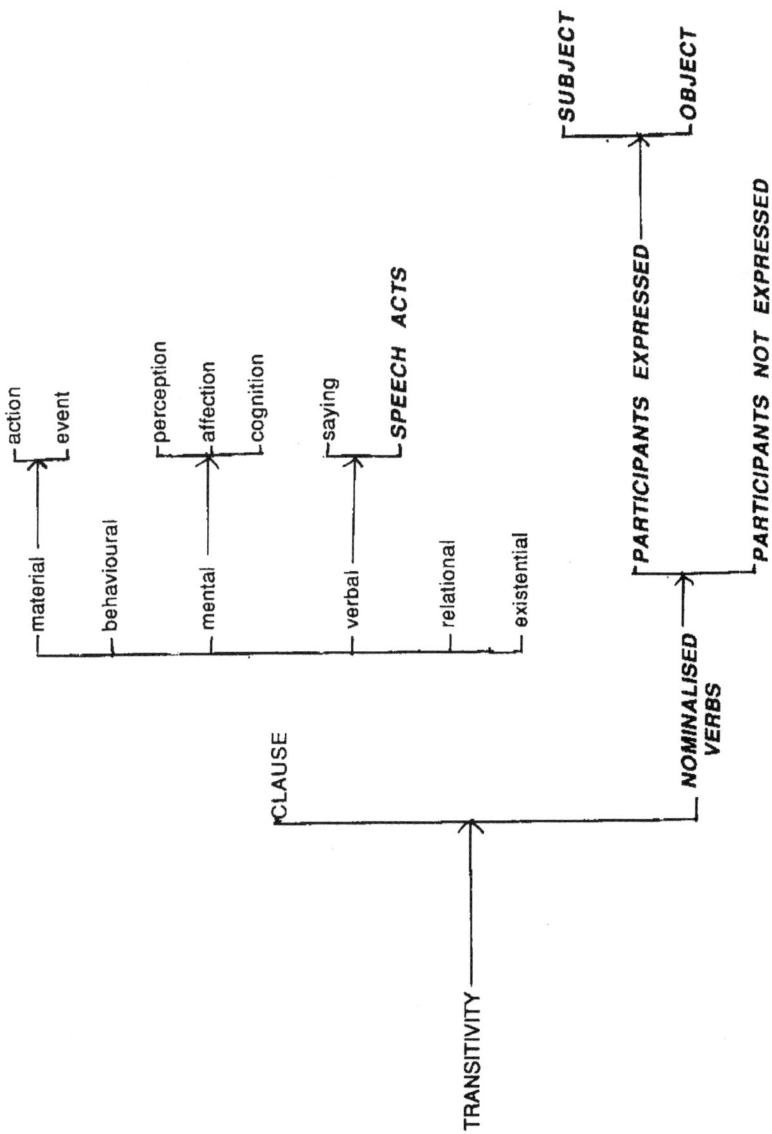

Mirror

MATERIAL ACTION PROCESSES

VERB	REALISATION	PARTICIPANTS	
		ACTOR	GOAL
treat	treatment	(doctors)	(patients)
heal	health	(doctors)	(patients)
serve	Service	(government)	(people)
operate	operation	(doctors)	(patients)
give	should give	they	operation
research	research	(doctors)	(patients)
help	can help	you	(Little B.)
treat	could be treated	(doctors)	whom (brave ten-year-old battling against leukaemia)
raise	to raise	appeal	cash
kill	killer	disease	(people)
affect	affects	disease	boys and girls such as Little B

MATERIAL EVENT PROCESSES

VERB	REALISATION	PARTICIPANTS	
		ACTOR	GOAL
Lat. nati – to be born	National	(people)	
begin	begins	brave Little B	
battle – to fight	battle (*METAPHOR*)		
live	life		
have a chance	has a slim chance	she	
pull through	can pull through	she	

RELATIONAL PROCESSES

VERB	REALISATION	PARTICIPANTS	
		IDENTIFIED	IDENTIFIER
be	was	she	the unnamed youngster denied... the NHS

MENTAL PERCEPTION PROCESSES

VERB	REALISATION	PARTICIPANTS	
		SENSER	PHENOMENON
hear	heard	she	her own case on the radio

MENTAL AFFECTION PROCESSES

VERB	REALISATION	PARTICIPANTS	
		SENSER	PHENOMENON
break	breaking (*METAPHOR*)	moment	heart
go out	went out (*METAPHOR*)	her heart	the girl in the news report

MENTAL COGNITION PROCESSES

VERB	REALISATION	PARTICIPANTS	
		SENSER	PHENOMENON
know	did not know	she	that she was the unnamed youngster denied treatment by the NHS
think	think		they should give her the operation
believe	believe		she can pull through

VERBAL PROCESSES

VERB	REALISATION	PARTICIPANTS	
		SAYER	TARGET
tell	told	father of cancer girl LB	of the heart-breaking moment on the radio
report	report	(reporter)	
tell	told	she	"I think they should give her the operation" **RECIPIENT**: her tearful dad
tell	told	her father	"I believe she can pull through"
insist	insisted	Dr. PG	RECIPIENT: *The Mirror*

SPEECH ACT PROCESSES

VERB	REALISATION	PARTICIPANTS	
		ACTOR	GOAL
name	unnamed	(reporter)	
deny	denied	NHS	treatment
appeal	appeal	Daily Mirror	cash
name	named	Daily Mirror	B Appeal
consult	consultant	(patients).	(doctors)

Guardian

MATERIAL ACTION PROCESSES

VERB	REALISATION	PARTICIPANTS	
		ACTOR	GOAL
heal	Health	(doctors)	(patients)
serve	Service	(government)	(people)
treat	treatment	(doctors)	(patients)
afford	cannot be afforded	public funds	which types of treatment
follow	should follow	Britain	the lead of the American state of Oregon which ... at public cost
lead	lead	Oregon	(anybody)
proceed	procedures	(doctors)	(patients)
avail	will not be available	public cost	medical procedures
cost	cost	(procedures)	(money)
govern	Government	(ministers etc.)	(people)
care	care	(doctors)	(patients)
ration	rationing	(government? doctors?)	(health care)
resist	have resisted	ministers	pressure

MATERIAL ACTION PROCESSES

VERB	REALISATION	PARTICIPANTS	
		ACTOR	**GOAL**
press	pressure	(Treasury?)	ministers
do	to do	(ministers)	an Oregon
leave	must be left	(ministers)	decisions
address	needs to be addressed	(government)	rationing issues
drive	is being driven	the ageing population, the links between high unemployment and ill-health and the increasing scope and sophistication of treatments	the demand for health care

MATERIAL EVENT PROCESSES

VERB	REALISATION	PARTICIPANTS	
		ACTOR	**GOAL**
span	spans (*METAPHOR*)	argument over explicit care rationing	the spectrum of political and medical opinion
suffer	sufferer	ten-year-old	leukaemia
increase	increasing (*METAPHOR*)	scope and sophistication of treatments	

MENTAL COGNITION PROCESSES

VERB	REALISATION	PARTICIPANTS	
		SENSER	PHENOMENON
L. scio to know	scientist		
show	show	his comments	that the argument the spectrum of political and medical opinion
opine	opinion	political and medical	

VERBAL PROCESSES

VERB	REALISATION	PARTICIPANTS	
		SAYER	TARGET
say	says	Sir D. B., former chief scientist at Dept of Health	The NHS should decide...
comment	comments	his	
criticise	criticising	Sir Douglas	The Govt's NHS market policies
argue	argument	political and medical opinion	over the case for ...rationing
say	say	ministers	decisions must be left to.... ... Cambridge health authority
say	say	Sir Douglas	the rationing issue ... available treatments

SPEECH ACT	PROCESSES		
VERB	**REALISATION**	**PARTICIPANTS**	
		ACTOR	**GOAL**
decide	should decide	NHS	which types of treatment... from public funds
declare	has declared	American state of Oregon	that more than one in six.... from public funds
decide	decisions	doctors at local level	
deny	denied	Cambridge health authority	treatment **RECIPIENT**: 10-year-old leukaemia sufferer
demand	demand	public	health care

APPENDIX F

BREAKTHROUGH TO LEARNING

BOOK 2

CONTENTS

Contents

GLOSSARY

This glossary explains only terms used without explanation in the main body of the paper. (The appendices contain additional terms which are clear in the context of the analyses.)

Examples are given in italics.

There are now many systems for describing the grammar of the clause. The definitions given here are derived from the Systemic Grammar associated with the work of M.A.K. Halliday.

Systemics describes language as a sets of options, from which the speaker chooses the ones appropriate to his/her meaning. Systems operate at every language level.

Examples from the level of the clause are given below under *mood* and *voice.*

Appendix E uses the transitivity system to analyse Texts A and B.

abstract — of the mind, dealing with ideas

active voice — See *voice.*

adjective — There are many classes of adjective. For the purposes of this paper an adjective is a word which describes a noun. (*The sky is* ***blue***)

adverb — See *part of speech.*

agent — This is Halliday's word for the doer of an action: it may be the subject of the active clause (***The visitor*** *dropped her bag.*) or follow *by* in a passive clause *The bag was dropped by* ***the visitor.***)

Halliday replaces the general word *agent* with other terms depending on the class of verb in the more refined description of the transitivity system used in Appendix E.

bilingual — knowing two languages. Now applied to learners who come to school having as a first language something other than English

clause There is more than one category of clause. Here we consider only the *major clause* – that is, a group of words with a subject, a verb and (optionally) an object. *I like peaches. – **Subject I, Verb like, Object** peaches.*

Clauses enter the systems of *mood, voice, transitivity* etc.

command See *mood*

complex sentences A complex sentence consists of more than one clause.

concept idea, named by an abstract noun (*thought, process, ability*)

concrete physical, having dimensions in space and time

creole A pidgin language which has become the mother tongue of a group of people.

derivation the origin of a word *The derivation of **energy** is the Greek verb ergon – to work.*

dialect A variety of language based on region. In England, regional dialects are identified with lower class speech.

discourse A particular style of speech or writing (*academic discourse*)

discourse analysis the rules for combining clauses or sentences into a text.

distance learning Learning materials prepared for students not in physical contact with a teacher. They used to be called 'correspondence courses'. The Open University is an example of distance learning

factor an element in the composition of an idea

feature A linguistic feature is any generalisable linguistic form at any level. For example, at clause level, the addition of *not* etc. is a linguistic feature signifying the negative.

form The *form* of a part of speech is the prefixes and/or suffixes which may be added to it and in terms of which its category is determined. For example, nouns may add the suffix *-s* to show they are plural.

function The *function* of a linguistic feature is the meaning it carries. For example, the formal addition of the suffix *ish* to an adjective carries the meaning *rather* – ***bluish***.

grammar in Systemic Grammar (as in traditional grammar), a description of the rules for combining words into clauses, and clauses into sentences. Traditionally divided into morphology and syntax

interjection *See part of speech*

metaphor an extension of meaning by which something is described as being that which it only resembles. *He is a* ***snake*** *in the* ***grass****, a* ***voyage*** *of self-discovery*

mood system

CLAUSE →
- indicative (statement) (*You are a teacher.*)
- interrogative (question) (*Are you a teacher?*)
- imperative (command) (*Be a teacher!*)

morpheme the basic unit of which words are made. They may be *free* – that is, they can stand alone (*bright, child, push*) or *bound* – that is, they have to be attached to a free morpheme. (*-ible, -ness, un-* etc.)

morphology the rules for combining morphemes into words

native speaker A native speaker of English is one who has English as his/her first language or mother tongue.

natural language the language of words etc. discussed here – as distinct from the 'languages' of music, dance, mathematics etc.

nominal group a group of words having the function of a noun ***The ringing of the bell*** *reminded them of their duties.*

nominalisation turning a verb or adjective into a noun (*consider* to *consideration, deep* to *depth*)

noun This is the part of speech that **names** an entity. It may be formally defined as having the option of putting *the* in front of it or of entering the system of **number** (singular or plural)

object The object of an active clause has the action done to it. *Hymie borrowed* ***the barrow****.*

paradigm Kuhn's word for a framework of ideas.

part of speech (or *word-class*). These are the categories of words which can enter the clause. See *noun, adjective, verb.* Other parts of speech are *adverb, interjection, pronoun, preposition, particle, prefix* etc.

particle See *part of speech.*

passive voice See *voice.*

past tense Verbs carry the time meaning of the clause – for example, present: *I play,* past: *I played,* future: *I shall play*

personification a branch of metaphor, in which an inanimate entity is referred to as a person (*the **aim** of analysis, the river **cuts** through the valley*)

pidgin a mixed language which develops when people speaking different languages come together for trade etc.

prefix See *part of speech.*

preposition See *part of speech.*

pronoun See *part of speech.*

question See *mood*

root a metaphoric expression for the earlier form of a word. (*The Latin verb fungi, functum is the **root** of the English word function*)

sentence The clause is the unit of the spoken language. The sentence is the unit of the written language It may consist of one or more clauses. Formally, it begins with a capital letter and ends with a full-stop.

Standard English A dialect of English which has the grammar of written English.

statement See *mood*

subject The subject of an active clause is the doer of the action. (***Phoebe** doesn't eat cake.*). It has the same number (singular or plural) as the verb. (***A bird** sings. **Birds** sing.*)

superlative This is a term in the system of degree:

ADJECTIVE → positive *happy* / comparative *happier* / superlative *happiest*

syntax a description of the rules for combining words into clauses and clauses into sentences

system (1) a set of options in Systemic Grammar. See *mood, voice* etc.

(2) something formed of parts which work together to make a whole, used especially here of variables acting together in a coherent way

text A text is a stretch of language, spoken or written, which can be regarded as having a coherent meaning, especially by the linguist intent on analysing it. It varies in length from one word – *Hi!* to *The Encyclopaedia Britannica.*

variable an abstract noun which names a concept. It may act with other variables to form a system.

variety A language *variety* is a particular style of language.

verb There are several classes of verbs, fully described in Appendix E. The most numerous are verbs of action, traditionally called *doing-words. The man* ***bit*** *the dog.* Verbs enter the systems of tense (present, past etc.) and person (*I, you, he* etc.)

vocabulary words

voice system

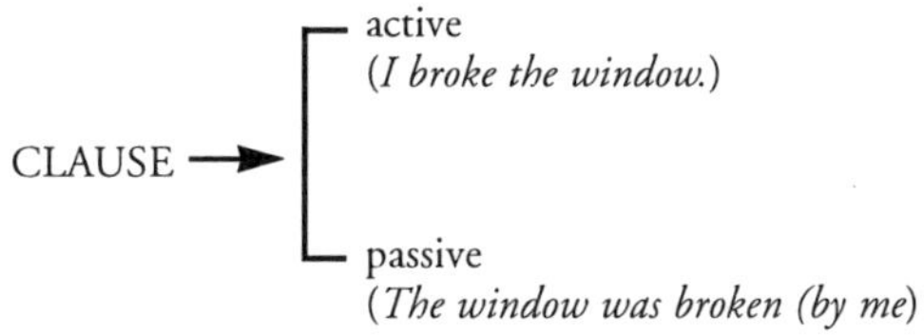

Bibliography

AUSTIN, J.L. (1962) *How To Do Things With Words*, Oxford: Clarendon Press

BERGER, PETER L. and LUCKMAN, THOMAS (1967) *The Social Construction of Reality*, London: Penguin

BERNSTEIN, BASIL (1959) A public language: some sociological implications of a linguistic form *British Journal of Sociology* 10, pp 311-326

BRAZIL, DAVID (1988) *The Communicative Value of Intonation in English*, University of Birmingham: Discourse Analysis Monograph, no. 8

BURTON, DEIRDRE D. (1982) 'Through Glass Darkly: Through Dark Glasses' in (ed.) CARTER, RONALD: *Language and Literature* (George Allen and Unwin)

BUZAN, TONY (1989) *Use your Head*, London, BBC

CHOMSKY, Noam (1968) *Language and Mind*, New York: Harcourt, Brace and World

CORSON, DAVID (1985) *The Lexical Bar*, Oxford, Pergamon

CUPITT, DON (1985) *Only Human*, SCM Press

DAVIES, FLORENCE AND GREENE, TERRY (1984) *Reading for Learning in the Sciences*, Edinburgh, Oliver and Boyd for the Schools Council

DES (1988) *Report of the Committee of Inquiry into the Teaching of English Language* (Kingman Report), HMSO

DES (1989) *National Curriculum: English for Ages 5 to 16* (Cox Report), HMSO

DOUGHTY, P., PEARCE, J. and THORNTON, G. (1971) *Language in Use*, London: Arnold

FAIRCLOUGH, NORMAN: (1989) *Language and Power*, London: Longman

FOUCAULT, MICHEL (1970) *The Order of Things*, trans. A. Sheridan. New York: Random House

FOWLER, H.W. (1926) *A Dictionary of Modern English Usage*, Oxford: Clarendon Press

GIBBONS, J. (1994) *Language and the Law*, London: Longman

HALLIDAY, M.A.K. (1973) *Explorations in the Functions of Language*, London: Arnold

HALLIDAY, M.A.K. (1984) *An Introduction to Functional Grammar*, London, Arnold

HEAP, BRIAN (1988) Teach English Proper!, *Link* (University of Lancaster Centre for Educational Research), Vol. 9, No. 1.

HEAP, BRIAN (1989) Wigan Language Project: Evaluation of the Language Awareness Course Illuminating English, Metropolitan Borough of Wigan (unpublished)

HELLAWELL, DAVID E. (1994) Education in Europe towards the twenty-first century in *International Journal of Educational Reform*, Technomic Publishing Company, Disk 1 Dr. 1 and 5 rc Jan '96 File HELLA

HMSO (1990) *LINC (Language in the National Curriculum)*

HOEY, MICHAEL (1983) *On the Surface of Discourse*, London, Allen and Unwin

JACKSON, HOWARD (1982) 'Errors of Punjabi Learners of English: a comparison of the grammars of Punjabi and English' in *I.T.L. Review of Applied Linguistics*, No. 55, pp 69-91

JOHNS, TIM (1996) *English for Academic Purposes*
Web, page http://sun 1.bham.ac.uk/johnstf/timeap3.htm

KUHN, THOMAS S. (1962) *The Structure of Scientific Revolutions*, Chicago: University Press

LABOV, W. (1972a) *Language in the Inner City*, Philadelphia: University of Philadelphia Press

LYONS, JOHN (1977) *Semantics*, Cambridge University Press

MASON, MARY (1986) The Deficit Hypothesis Revisited, *Educational Studies*, Vol. 12, No. 3.

MASON, MARY (1987) The Linguistic Mechanisms of Abstract Thought, *ITL Review of Applied Linguistics*, 75, pp 1-35

MASON, MARY (1988a) *Illuminating English Book 1: Language Awareness* (TRACE Wigan)

MASON, MARY (1988b) A Language Awareness Project in Wigan, in ed. BRUMFIT, CHRISTOPHER *Language in Teacher Education*, National Congress on Languages in Education, pp 126-127

MASON, MARY (1989) *Illuminating English Book 2: Reading for Learning* (TRACE Wigan)

MASON, MARY (1990a) *Illuminating English Book 3: Writing for Learning* (TRACE Wigan)

MASON, MARY (1990b) Dancing on Air: An Analysis of a Passage from an Economics Textbook in DUDLEY-EVANS, TONY and HENDERSON, WILLIE (eds.) *ELT Documents 134*, Modern English Publications and the British Council, pp 16-28

MASON, MARY (1995a) 'Language for Learning at Bordesley Green Girls' School' in *Multi-Cultural Education Review*, Birmingham City Council, no. 17, Winter Term 1995/96

MASON, MARY (1995b) *Breakthrough to Learning: Book 1: Language Awareness* (Wigan and Leigh College)

MASON, MARY and SANDLAND, JOAN (1996) 'Breakthrough to Learning: a Course in Language across the Curriculum' in SUBHI, ZORA (ed): *Bridging the Gap between Theory and Practice in the Teaching of English as an Additional Language* (papers from the first and second conferences on ESL held at Small Heath School, Birmingham, 1994 and 1995)

MASON, MARY (1996) *Breakthrough to Learning: Book 2: Reading for Learning* (Wigan and Leigh College)

McCLOSKEY, DONALD C. (1986) *The Rhetoric of Economics*, Brighton, Wheatsheaf Books Ltd.

MYERS,GREG (1990) *Writing Biology: Text in the Social Construction of Scientific Knowledge*, Madison, US.A, University of Wisconsin Press

PEREIRA, KATHARINE (1979) The language demands of school learning, in Open University course P232, block 6 *Language development*

SAUSSURE, F. DE (1916) Cours de Linguistique Générale, Paris: Payot (English translation by Wade, Baskin: *Course in General Linguistics*, New York: Philosophical Library, 1959)

SWALES, JOHN (1990) *Genre Analysis: English in Academic and Research Settings*, Cambridge, Cambridge University Press

TOOLAN, MICHAEL (forthcoming) 'What is Critical Discourse Analysis and why are they saying such terrible things about it?', *Language and Literature*

WIDDOWSON, H.G. (ed.) (1980) *Reading and Thinking in English: Discovering Discourse,* Oxford, Oxford University Press

WILLIS, DAVE (1990) *The Lexical Syllabus: a New Approach to Language Teaching*, Harper Collins

WINTER, EUGENE (1978) *A look at the role of certain words in information structure* (From K.P. JONES and V. HORSNELL Informatics 3, (London, ASLIB)

WINTER, EUGENE (1986) Clause Relations as Information Structure: Two Basic Structures in English (in MALCOLM COULTHARD (ed.) *Talking about Text*, ELR Discourses Monograph No. 13. (Birmingham, University of Birmingham)